# 14 ways to reignite the spark in your relationship.

## Keeping the passion alive.

By

## Dr TIMOTHY KESSINGTON.

approval from the publisher or creator.

# TABLE OF CONTENTS

# TABLE OF CONTENT

**Conclusion:**

# ABOUT THE AUTHOR

**Dr. TIMOTHY KESSINGTON** is a licensed psychologist in the state of texas. he is a certified counselor on marriage and relationship/mental health. He is passionate to the core to see people in relationships happy and couples achieve the best out of every relationship

**Introduction:**

Relationships are an important part of our lives and require constant care and attention. Despite our best efforts, the spark in our relationships can sometimes fizzle out, leaving us feeling disconnected and unfulfilled. Fortunately, with a little effort and dedication, you can rekindle the spark in your relationship. In this book, we will look at 14 different ways to rekindle the spark in your relationship, beginning with defining what the spark is and why it is so important to your relationship.

# CHAPTER 1

## What is the Spark.

The initial attraction, chemistry, and excitement that people feel when they first meet and begin a relationship is referred to as the spark. This sensation is frequently accompanied by butterflies in the stomach, intense passion, and a strong emotional bond.

# CHAPTER 2

## Why is the Spark Important.

The spark is necessary because it establishes the foundation for a healthy and fulfilling relationship. It fosters emotional intimacy and keeps the relationship fresh and exciting by creating a sense of excitement and anticipation.

# Chapter 3:

## Identifying the Issue.

The first step in rekindling the flame in your relationship is to identify the source of the problem. Spend some time reflecting on what has gone wrong and discussing your concerns with your partner.

# CHAPTER 4

## Communicate.

Communication that is open and honest is essential in any successful relationship. Without passing judgment, express your feelings and listen to your partner's concerns.

# CHAPTER 5

## Spend Quality Time Together.

Spending quality time together is essential for rekindling the flame in your relationship. Make time for each other regularly and plan fun activities that you both enjoy.

# CHAPTER 6

## Discover New Interests Together.

Exploring new hobbies together can help you reconnect and reinvigorate your relationship. Try something new that both of you enjoy, such as cooking, hiking, or painting.

# CHAPTER 7

## Show Appreciation and Affection.

Showing your appreciation and affection for your partner is a simple yet effective way to rekindle the flame in your relationship. Every day, make an effort to show them how much you care.

# CHAPTER 8

## Surprise Each other.

Keeping your relationship exciting and fresh by surprising your partner with thoughtful gestures and gifts. Plan a surprise date night for your partner or leave a sweet note for them to find.

# CHAPTER 9

## Try Something New in the Bedroom.

Spiking things up in the bedroom can help to rekindle the fire in your relationship. Try out new positions, toys, and fantasies.

# CHAPTER 10

## Practice Gratitude.

Practicing gratitude can help you improve your relationship and reignite the flame. Take time to appreciate the positive aspects of your relationship and thank your partner.

# CHAPTER 11

## Emphasis on Self-Care.

Self-care can make you feel more confident and fulfilled in your relationship. Maintain your physical, emotional, and mental well-being, and encourage your partner to do the same.

# CHAPTER 12

## Learn Each Other's Love Languages.

Understanding each other's love languages can assist you in expressing your love and appreciation in ways that are meaningful to your partner. Make an effort to learn each other's love languages and express love in those ways.

# CHAPTER 13

## Seek Professional Assistance.

Seeking professional help if you're struggling to rekindle the spark in your relationship can be beneficial. Consider couples therapy or counseling to help you work through problems and strengthen your relationship.

# CHAPTER 14

## Exercise Patience and Persistence.

It takes time and effort to rekindle the flame in your relationship. Don't give up on your relationship; instead, practice patience and perseverance.

## Conclusion:

With a little effort and dedication, you can rekindle the flame in your relationship. Identifying the issue, communicating openly, spending quality time together, exploring new hobbies, expressing appreciation and affection, trying something new in the bedroom, and practicing gratitude are all ways to help.